Patsy Cline is on the Radio

For Lesily
who heals the
body and mind
and has a larger
vocabulary than
I do —
Enjoy!

poems by

Barbara Dahlberg

Barbara

Finishing Line Press
Georgetown, Kentucky

Patsy Cline is on the Radio

ACKNOWLEDGMENTS

Grateful acknowledgment is given to the editors of the following publications in which
these poems first appeared (some in different form);
Lascaux Prize 2016: "Bartlesville, Oklahoma 1980"
Pittsburgh Poetry Review: "The Stars are Different"
U.S.1 Worksheets Volume 59: "The Doctor Said"
Voices from the Attic, Volume XV111: "The bottle blonde," and "Survivor"
Voices from the Attic, Volume XIX: "Drawing Home," and "Fayetteville,
Arkansas, December 26, 1979"
Voices from the Attic, Volume XXI: "The All Meat Diet," and "Oklahoma"

Thank you to:

My Madwomen in the Attic teachers: Jan Beatty, Nancy Krygowski, and Stacey Waite for
pushing me to dig deep and explore, to Liane Ellison Nelson for mentoring me, to Valerie
Bacharach for her laser eye and tender ear, to my fellow Madwomen for listening with
honesty and tact, to my surgeons Dr. Pingpank, Dr. Schuchert and Dr. Jacobs, for keeping
me alive, to my oncologist Dr. Bahary for always asking, "Do you want the good news or
the bad news first?" to the nurses and Michelle at Hillman Cancer Center for being my
second family, to my friends and family who have chanted, prayed and sung to heal me,
provided rides, clean laundry, fresh scones, and kept me laughing, to Jim and Tina Kirsch
for coming to every chemo, to Rachael Nuwash for six months of daily affirmations, to
my three glorious sisters, Kathy Short, Patricia Cohan and Priscilla Nuwash, for being the
tripod that supported me through the darkest times, and finally to my son Zach for never,
ever doubting me.

Publisher: Leah Maines
Editor: Christen Kincaid
Cover Art: Barbara Dahlberg
Photo of Cover Art: Priscilla Nuwash
Author Photo: Scott Smith
Cover Design: Elizabeth Maines McCleavy

Printed in the USA on acid-free paper.
Order online: www.finishinglinepress.com
                also available on amazon.com

Author inquiries and mail orders:
Finishing Line Press
P. O. Box 1626
Georgetown, Kentucky 40324
U. S. A.

Table of Contents

Four

Acknowledgments

I'd like to dedicate this book to my mother
Veronica Augustyn Dahlberg, July 1925 – May 1975,
a true warrior.

One

The Stars are Different

In a cemetery near campus,
a frigid January night,
snow mounded, sky black.
A boy shows me Orion's belt,
head formed by the seven sisters.

Years later my younger son,
a Marine on a secret mission,
sails towards Iraq.
His earth curves away from me.

I asked him if he saw dolphins, whales,
or those birds that never land.
He laughed,
said he never had time
for sky, for water,
just got greasy
fixing helicopters.

Stationed in Ar-Rutbah.
The wind blows
in every direction,
sandstorms last a week.
He got along with people
he couldn't get away from.
Has stories he doesn't tell.

Happy Talk

They don't expect her to live
after the mastectomy.
She's thirty and has five children
(the oldest is seven)
cared for by a series of aunts,
grandmothers, and friends.

Too young to visit the hospital
we wave from the parking lot.
She stands in the window.
My oldest sister toilet trains me
using Cheerios as the treat.

Skin harvested from her stomach
stretches thin over ribs
where her left breast used to be.
Her arm is always swollen.
My baby sister learns to cling
to my mother's back
to get out to the crib.

Glamour in the 50's
means girdles and pearls.
A beauty, she wears red lipstick
starched white shirts tucked
into dirndl skirts to do laundry.

Her prosthetic breast chafes,
never fits right.
My father takes endless movies
a chronicle of little bodies
in constant motion.
My mother ducks out of every frame.

We have little money
but for Christmas that year
my mother gets a piano

to strengthen her arm.
She plays and my parents sing
Rogers and Hammerstein's
Bali Hi and *Happy Talk*.

Minnesota Summer

Dirt path into the woods
full of rainbow colored toadstools
ticks and tiny May flowers.
We crouch for hours by mossy stumps
rotted into crenelated castles.
Bug bitten, hair snarly
crowned with twigs and leaves.

Oklahoma, April 1981

I married a man
who couldn't be a husband
refused to be a father.
Rocks run in my family.
I stayed.

We sang duets in the red Datsun truck
Little Feat songs- *Sailin Shoes, Dixie Chicken*,
dog Buddy between us.
Picked peyote in the deserts.
Moved west or south to some new town
he'd heard about-
Nacogdoches, Twin Falls, Durango.

Never north where my people were.

We stayed in Oklahoma for a year.
Everything bites or stings.
I'd get midnight calls
from the drunk tank in some small town
as the creek beds rang with a coyote devil chorus.
I'd borrow money, find a ride,
bail him out.

I was alone the day the tornados leveled
Wichita Falls, Texas.
I jerked storm cellar door open.
A huge snake slithered out.
A black widow over the entrance,
scorpion on the steps.
Back in the house I crouched in the bathtub
with my dog until the storm passed.

When my son was born I tried to leave.
He came home in the middle of the day.
I waited a few weeks and left again
with just a diaper bag,
hid in the bathroom until my flight was called
nursed my son as we flew over the red dirt.

Solome

Great grandmother Solome
dirt on her name
dirt thrown on an empty coffin.

Hid in a hay wagon.
Fled her family
fled the pogroms

to marry a Catholic boy.
Gambled Krakow for
Wisconsin's black dirt.

Mother of nine died early
gifted four generations
red hair and cancer.

At the Dig, Gaswell, Pennsylvania

Two intact graves, once heaped with flowers
hold the skeletons of two young women

cradling newborns—surrounded by essentials
for the next life: bone fish hooks, pottery, a puppy.

They face west, knees bent, left arms pointing north.
Wear shell necklaces strung to look like blossoms.

Who are these women, vanished for centuries?
The team studies, measures, places them in coffins.

The Seneca tribe from upstate New York claim the bones.

Humming Aretha's *Respect* while walking the hallways of Clayton Elementary, Pittsburgh, PA

Stepping down the long tan hallway
a soul tune from *WAMO* in my head
Aretha Franklin testifying to the world.
1998, I hear her echo down city alleys.

90% of the students in the classrooms I pass are Black—
neat cornrows that end in bright ballies, clean Adidas sneakers,
half the staff is too.
I am the white art teacher.

Chauncey, a sixth grader,
holds his thumb and finger a 1/4 inch apart,
tells me, *My Dad used a belt this thick after you phoned my house.*
There is no change in his behavior.

I silence my head.

You can make a difference! I tell myself.
One cold recess in February, my favorite second grader,
shivering, leans into me and I wrap my coat around us both.
His teeth are rotted.
In the background I see the city skyline.

Open windows bring sweet May breezes.
I hear second grade girls chant,
Miss Mary Mack, Mack, Mack...
Skipping rope slaps asphalt.
Girls shriek as boys chase

along the high chain link fence.
Hoop shots twang
balance for a moment on the rim.
The bell rings.

Crows

No songs, just call and response. Like
clots of teenaged boys, not to be trusted.

They clack their beaks in greeting. Study
the white garbage bags, strew bones and juice-

soaked papers. Fly so high their black wings
look white under the winter sun. Massing

at dusk like flecks of pepper drawn down
in a current towards Homewood Cemetery.

Christmas at Western Psych

I learn to work the system to keep him safe
if only for a week or two.
I lie: *He threatened me, he's suicidal.*
He says he'll stay this time until they fix him.

This visit is better.
They search us, open the wrapped presents.
We chat and laugh, Jesse plays host.
He takes me aside, shows me a book
with a secret hollow cut in the center.
What did it hold?

I'm nervous, afraid that something will start a fight.
I need to feel in control so I say, *It's time to go home,*
regret it immediately.
It's the last time we are together,
his brother back to Pensacola
his father back to Butler.

Two

The Ginger Jar

You keep your son's ashes close
in a red velvet pouch.
My son's are in a ginger jar
on top of a tall cabinet
at his brother's house.

You remember his smile and humor—
I remember how angry everyone was.
You think of those ashes as his heart,
his lungs, his skin, hair.

The jar is so heavy.

I want to pry the lid off the jar
plunge my hand in
feel for shards of bone
taste my fingers.

The bottle blonde

with Wonder Bread breasts

leans over

taps my arm.

"What's your name?

I want to pray for you."

Pray for the kids in Somalia

better yet buy them a goat.

I paid fifty bucks to

hear Lucinda Williams sing,

not to be reminded.

You think I should be grateful

thrilled to be bald and 20 pounds heavier.

Just add me to your list and I'm sure

your god will fix everything.

Meanwhile, give your self a pat on the back

and leave me alone.

The All Meat Diet

The chemo every other week is good poison
tingles my extremities, turns my palms
and the bottoms of my feet brown.
It makes food taste like dirty pennies.
Gives me Einstein brows.
Meat tastes good with a layer of bacon.

Spent my lifetime eating the right foods.
I still got sick.
Maybe from a gene or the fumes
from painting houses 30 years ago.
We used sludge full of heavy metals
to fertilized our garden, ate unwashed peaches
hot and sweet right from the tree.

The open sewers in our neighborhood
turn out to have been good for kids,
built the immune system
unless you got polio
like Timmy-with-the-brace
from down the street.

Not so good were hot dogs and Kool-Aid
laced with red dye #5,
bikes ridden in the fog behind the mosquito truck,
or later, weed from Mexico doused with paraquat.

Are There Separate Heavens?

Is it enough, I ask my Muslim friend
to be a good person?
Is it fair that she must be covered head to toe
in 100 degree heat while her husband wears shorts?
Why is she unclean after he touches her?

She assures me that her reward in heaven
will be so much better than mine.
Everything she suffers on earth
will make it worth while.

What Saves Us

Breathe in,
through panic
through dark
surface, go under,
long halls, bright lights,
nurses, needles,
morphine.

Breathe in, breathe out
reach, stroke, turn head, exhale
breathe in, turn head, reach,
stroke, exhale.

Breathe in,
crossword puzzles,
channel surfing,
oatmeal, Sudoko,
chicken-pot-pies,
chemo.

Breathe in, breathe out,
air cold, then warm,
toads return, mate,
plant flowers,
dead head roses,
count steps,
laps,
miles.

All winter I wear a

cavernous mink coat freed
from a Goodwill box in an alley.

Heavy as a bear,
long enough to lick my calves.

Curly white lamb boa
winds around my throat.

On my head a magenta cloche
anchored with a fake diamond pin.

On an Art Department trip
to New York City, we walk miles.

February grey sleet rides on my shoulders.
In the warm subway matted fur begins to

waft feral. I catch Gary from Art History
staring.

I know he wants me.

Dolores Means Sadness

We drove all day through the desert
spent the night in a cheap hotel
in Dolores, Colorado
with patterned wallpaper and aqua tile.
Red light from the vacancy sign
buzzed and leaked into the room
around the edges of the torn shade.

The air conditioner rattled and droned
unbearably loud,
blew frigid air until we shut it off
only to wake again,
each in our own trench.

Terri with an i, Dotted with a Heart

Shimmy-ing across a ravine on a 12" gas pipe
in the dark, following Lee DePew to a field

just for sex, in the era of free love, that wasn't.
No toothbrush, no tent, no stars. It starts to rain.

He's still in love with my roommate Terri.
Terri with an i, dotted with a heart.

The Dead

A fragment of talk radio
blows my body out of bed.
I weigh-in at 6:30 while brushing my teeth.
Stand for 6 seconds on the cold glass scale,
wait for numbers to stop blinking.
Without glasses I have to crouch to see
how many of the last 5 pounds
have come or gone again.
Newspaper waits outside the door.
I skim headlines,
ignore sports, pause at photos
of the recently dead.
Lacquered hair, cat-eye glasses,
pearls, part of a lover's arm.
Heads tilt, look out of the frame.
Loved animals.
Collected tools.

She Takes a Stand on Jello

I'm home!
He waits at the door for his two girls,
the last of his five, to greet him with a kiss.
He can hear the older girl laughing.
His eyes follow the springy yellow phone cord
stretched tight as it disappears behind the bathroom door.
The youngest stays in her room.

He turns on the t.v.—flickery scenes of helicopters.
Palm branches switch wildly.
Young men in camouflage crouch under whirring blades.
CBS News joins the table.

Through dinner the two girls make eye contact in the mirror
behind their mother's head.
Find everything he says so funny,
they laugh until milk shoots out their noses.
He looks hard at the older girl,
sees her for the first time,
smudged blue eyeliner,
newly pierced ears red and swollen,
hair bleached *Summer Blonde.*
Watches as she pushes food around her plate.

Eat your jello.
She stares at her the cherry jello, melt-y,
pooling into the catsup and meat juice.
She meets his eyes.
No.
Her mother hisses, *You"ll give your father a heart attack.*
Even her sister is shocked.

Walter Cronkite's voice drones in the background
as he reads the names and ages of the newly dead.

Bartlesville, Oklahoma, 1980

The summer before you were born
was the hottest in 100 years.
With no place to go your father and I
moved into a tiny white farmhouse
with his sister Jean.

We overstayed our welcome
by at least two months.

The garden shriveled and burned
no matter how much I watered.
Under the straw mulch lay toads
splayed and bloated with water.
Locusts came and ate the few surviving plants,
even flew off with my dog Buddy's food,
nugget by nugget.

The wind blew red grit
onto every surface, into every bite we ate
sitting on webbed lawn chairs
in the living room
after Jean moved out,
took the tables
the couch
and the T.V.
Before she left her dog killed Buddy.

Alone in the evenings,
I sat on the porch swing
holding my belly
waiting for a breeze.
Birds nested on top
the rotten wooden pillars.
Beaks and bird bones
poked from holes

near the bottom.
Every night I watched
the taillights recede
as plumes of dust followed
your Dad to the bar.
I'd find him in the morning
face down in the dirt
somewhere between the porch steps
and the open truck door.

Letters home described
scissor-tailed flycatchers,
magical skies where stars
touched the ground,
the Milky Way a solid path.

Thank You for Your Service

On deck, he watches for specks to become flying machines.
Hunches under blurred blades, fixes Viet Nam era copters
that break down each time they fly.

Sea and sky, sea and sky—nothing but grey.
Canned food for weeks.
Plastic garbage melted into disks, tossed in the sea.

Early morning Suez Canal, flattest water he's ever seen
mirrors the sky and rocky sand.
Poles and lights strung on both sides vanish to a point
in the distance.

Every so often he sees a guy standing in the middle
of nowhere pointing a gun at him.
Dunes and rocks, rocks and dunes
missile launchers big as cars.
A mosque in the shape of an AK 47.

Tuesday is surf and turf day at Al Assad
base in Iraq. Chefs in toques and checkered
pants serve lobster and steak.

On Rumsfield's birthday there's a cake six feet
long and four feet high shaped like the Taj Mahal.
No one eats it.

There's a Pizza Hut nearby.

Moments after leaving the latrine, a bomb
lobbed over the fence kills the guy in the
stall to his left, blows the legs off the guy
on his right.

Three

The Doctor Said

In a worst case scenario
you have five months to live.

Does that start right now?
Can it start tomorrow?
What about February?
It's only 28 days.
How does that figure in?

What can I do in 5 months?
Organize drawers.
Say thank you.
Eat everything
I ever wanted.
Spend money?
Should I sleep?

Who to tell?
Is it worse to know?
Maybe he said it to make me mad.
Or he could be crazy.
Why tell me at all?

I try to visualize a healthy liver,
whatever that looks like.
Pink I guess.
Busy doing liver things,
like filtering my last Guinness.
tending to the Merlot.

The Juice King

We were young when my parents died.
Our step-mother let each take a few things:
Pat got the piano, Kathy the silver, Bob the china,
Scilla the sewing machine.
I chose a box of rocks and the Juice King.
The wooden box held: a tawny sandstone
with the impression of a perfect gingko leaf
a black rock with milky blue flashes,
hollow agates with amethyst hearts,
fossilized crinoid.
The Juice King is squat
with chipped white paint
a shiny chrome helmet that covers
a galvanized ribbed cone.
Lower the arm on a citrus half
juice squishes out.
I chew the pulpy rinds.
My lips tingle.

**Aunt Lorraine squeezes through the bathroom window
to grab the jewelry after Great Aunt Martha dies.**

We visit once a year. The house smells like rotting
bananas. It is too hot. Great Aunt Martha
promises us each a piece of jewelry when she dies.

She wears lots of jewelry, turquoise stones in heavy
tarnished silver, squash blossom necklaces, rings
and bracelets with coral and obsidian inlays.

She lets me look through her junk drawer.
I admire a bag of petrified frosting roses, a doll
sized violin, three diamond rings on a diaper pin.

Martha never married. Once a beauty,
pale skin, long red hair, piled on her head.
She taught at an Indian school in Tucson.

In a photo she smiles, surrounded by her solemn
students, braids shorn, dressed in Anglo clothes.
Saguaro cacti reach for the sky.

My younger sister gets a dollar after she says
she wants to be a nun when she grows up.
As we leave, Martha leans in.

We kiss her wrinkly powdered face,
lipstick stuck to her teeth,
rouge on only one cheek.

On Facebook

your old girlfriend
wanted to friend me.
She was the one that taught you
to hide the tracks
between your toes.

You were always so afraid
of needles.

She is married.
Has a blonde baby.
You are dead.

Big Weather

My mother leads us down the wooden
steps to the unfinished basement.
We pray. She lights a
Holy candle.
After the storm our
father cuts birch bark from
toppled trees. We sew tiny canoes.

Outside of Albuquerque, December 21, 1982

The day my father died I made a journey
with my new husband and two-year-old son
to the high desert behind
the Cochiti Indian Reservation.
Desolate lunar landscape
a few scrubby pinon pines.
Stellar Jays with floppy topknots call a warning.

Surrounded by hoodoos,
the A-bomb shaped sand and rock formations
taller than my 6'7" husband,
we bend to look for Apache tears.
Lucky to find the obsidian pebbles
tumbled smooth in the dry wash.

Back at the apartment
the phone rings and rings
rattles the windows
ricochets off the tile floors
as my sisters call
to tell me our father is dead.

My father with the beaky nose
droplet of sweat trembling on the tip
as he sawed through lumber.
Geologist and funny man with lame jokes
worn down like glass by a job he hated,
never enough money.

I sit in the dirt with my son
counting the days until my own surgery
to remove both breasts at age 29,
the surgery my 3 sisters and 3 cousins will all have
in hopes of cheating the cancer gene that killed
my mother and her identical twin at 49.

I don't go to his funeral
choose not to witness
my step-mother staring into the open grave.

In the Onion Drawer

Fragile layers hold fast.
Houdini-like green shoots

bend double, push and strain
against the papery skin.

A misshapen, oddly beautiful
harbinger of spring.

Pepperoni, Bedpans, and Polyester

I crease pizza boxes in the down times
create a leaning tower to stand behind.
The skinny owner pretends to read the newspaper,
sticking his butt into the aisle.
I squeeze by.
I love the walk-in, eat pepperoni
and canned mushrooms by the handful,
emerge, wipe my mouth with the back of my hand.
I poke yesterday's hard mozzarella worms
out of the grinder with a screwdriver bit.
The pizzas are delivered half-baked,
square, and stacked loosely draped in plastic.
I quit when he slides a hand over my breast.

Urine smells sting my nose.
Patients tied and slumped in wheelchairs moan.
I learn to change sheets on a bed
with someone still in it.
I empty catheters, pull hair
from wheelchair spokes.
One patient chases me around the room
swinging a bag of oranges yelling, *Stop thief!*
They all want to talk,
tell stories of marriage at 13,
how to churn butter, butcher a sow.
One man explains how he split stones
for cathedrals and bridges.
I wear a white uniform.
I try to be kind.

I learn to fold in one fluid motion. Shirts
embalmed in chemicals make my nose twitch.
The Blue Light Specials cause a stampede.
Nobody speaks to me as they paw
through mounds of slippery polyester
on the bargain table at K-Mart. I repair the damage,
fold and refold through the hot hours from 6-10 p.m.

Afternoon Delight by The Starland Vocal Band
and *Levon* by Elton John mark the beginning
and end of the Muzak loop.
I flirt with the oboe player from Garden Supplies.
I'll be gone with the mulch and bathing suits.

You Said

I love you like the wind.
What is that supposed to mean?
Hardly terms of endearment
more like a curse.
Unlike a breeze
the wind gives nothing
shears off small pieces
scours and reddens.
Restless thing that presses close
then greedy and cold
snatches what it wants.

Fayetteville, Arkansas, December 26, 1977

I have never liked fruitcake

but I remember eating pieces

broken from the loaf

my sister sent.

Bits stuck to my fingers

my clothes

as I tried to taste Christmas.

I lived with my husband Danny

in a shack of a house.

Shafts of sunlight

poked through the walls.

Had to step over a frozen stream

when the neighbor's toilet

backed up in the yard.

Danny had been gone for two days.

Alone with my sister's fruitcake

I stuffed my mouth

chewed and swallowed

chewed and swallowed.

Didn't taste it

couldn't cry

as I ate it all

nuts and raisins

bits of pineapple

and dried cherries.

The sticky cake

coated my teeth.

No money to leave

nowhere to go.

I couldn't tell my people

how unbelievably,

unbearably,

helpless I felt

eating fruitcake

on my birthday

and gagging.

Four

My Bohemian Grandmother

Red, knuckly, painful hands
that mended, sewed and washed,
worked the seasons, planting and canning
the harvest, feeding the animals
that in return fed us.

No waste in her kitchen.
Leftovers from one meal
appeared at the next,
new onions that bit back, radishes,
sweet pickles, eye-watering horseradish.

Meat at every meal.
Sometimes summer sausage,
pungent, garlicky, flecked
with lard and whole peppercorns,
sliced from a log the width of a man's arm.

Scraps to the chickens and massive pig,
dishwater to the garden.
Ashes and grease united in alchemy,
became thick slabs of yellow soap
for hair, hands, and laundry.

The cast iron stove,
shiny and smooth with wear
never went out, stoked with wood
split with the same axe
that cut the heads off chickens.
The kitchen always smelled faintly
of past meals, wood smoke,
fierce coffee that simmered
in a blue enameled pot,
ready to fill the cups of my grandfather
and his workmen.

Her hands kneaded and mixed dough
for bread seasoned with dill and caraway.
Kolaches filled with prunes, berries or poppy seeds.

With Love

Don't forget to brush your teeth
and believe I have always wanted
what was best for you.
When I counted your fingers, your toes,
saw you were perfect
I figured we had it made.
Everything would be alright,
but the nature of the beast
was only hidden.
With a few states behind us
no forwarding address
you were mine to shape and pull.

Stage 4 Cancer

Sleep, wake, dreamless
I have a life but everything
is gone or changed.
My torso cut
spliced back imperfectly,
brain fuzzy and overexposed
in a chemical bath.
My body that gave so much
no longer bends.
The reflection in the mirror
is the image of a stranger.
The what ifs don't become me.

On the Farm

Two lane dirt roads straight and long
bisect the rich Wisconsin land bordered by cornfields.
We share comic books on the long drive
from northern Minnesota in a station wagon
named the Green Hornet.

The farms have house, garden, silo, barn.
Pink and blue lupine in the ditches.
Black and white Holsteins stud the fields like
peppercorns in summer sausage.

The massive sow even eats live chickens.
Smothering piles of oats.
Silo full of methane gas.
Aunt Lorraine is nice for the first few days.

Twice a day we stand apart.
Watch the cow parade to and from the barn.
The milk machines chug the milk away in long tubes.
We love it when the cows poop.

My Mother Never Flew Solo

Before marriage at twenty-four
she helped build B-52 bombers.
She wanted to be a doctor and a pilot
instead earned a teaching degree in Biology
spent the money for her last pilot lesson
on a new dress.

Her thick dark hair curls in the damp steam
as she uses a long stick to fish laundry
out of the Maytag wringer washer.
Feeds the sodden mass into the yellowed
rolling jaws that gape and squeal
as water gushes out.

She pulls towels through,
flattened and embedded with tiny socks.
The clothes are hung on a line outside,
where they freeze in the Minnesota winter.

Tarzan's Cry

Dad sits on a hay bale throne—
my brother, three sisters and I
lounge on our bellies at his feet.
He tells us stories he's memorized
of the white man in Africa wrestling snakes,
fighting cannibals, saving Jane.

He is a softer, not so handsome Johnny Wiessmuller:
straight black hair Brylcreemed into a Midwest pompadour.
Grey-blue eyes squint behind Clark Kent glasses
as he yodels Tarzan's cry.
Startled pigeons dart from the rafters.

The barn is mostly empty today
lit by sparkly dust-moted sun shafts.
Faintly green, grassy smelling hay
is stacked to the ceilings in some places.
Tomorrow a crew of sweaty men
lead by our dour grandfather
will unload the trucks.
A huge iron claw, lowered by ropes
will grasp the bales and swing them into place.
Open spaces obliterated
filled with noise and activity
but today the cathedral is ours.

Clever man, my dad
in the boredom and the July heat
keeps us from the kitchen
where our mom and her mother
bond over pie crusts.
Keeps us safe from sharp tongued Aunt Lorraine
the music teacher who hates kids.

My dad is not a handsome man but knows how to laugh.
A mining engineer, he intersperses the stories
with details about fossils, igneous rocks and plate tectonics.
Odd useless facts but our inheritance just the same.

Mercy Hospital, April 1975

Breaths gentle,
lines smoothed from her face.
I knew.

I eat her lunch,
but not the neon green peas
wrinkling in the tray.

Tubes in her nostrils.
Bags drip fluid in.
Bag traps yellow pee.

My mother halved.
Shaft of light
glints off a spoon.

Survivor

Still myself—
hollow but meaty

Sturdy feet
  detour
down tear trails
  slick and salty

Imagine
  a lake
ripples reversed
  rock
returns to hand

Your First Breath a Wail

Overtaken by an urge
to lick and clean your body—
an animal mother.
I inhale your scent.
Nose in your downy
golden folds.

A cuddler, the nurse cooed,
we've got a cuddler here,
as she carried you away.

I dreamt of you
body tensed
poised over the chasm.
Too heavy for the slender branch
that bowed under your weight.

My hands reach and grasp empty air.

Drawing Home

It looks insubstantial
    unfinished
like if you pushed hard enough
it would collapse

a treasure trove
of what didn't work—
dreams with no sticking point
flowers that want
to sketch themselves
into blossoms

This is hope.
The steps bigger
than the mountains
    start here
end somewhere else.

Patsy Cline is on the Radio

I was in charge—
the only one of the of the 4 sisters still at home.
My feelings preserved in salt.
I pushed away, packed, and tossed
everything my mother owned.
No one asked about her clothes, her shoes—
no one told me.

I had never been to a funeral.
We buried her in a magenta dress
with a paisley design, hand-me-down
from her best friend's rich cousin.
Close the casket.
No aunties to rock me as I wailed and grieved.
No old bones to visit, no religion at 22.

Only 49 when she lost
her thick-as-a-horse's tail brown hair.
She wanted to talk about dying
but I wouldn't.
With oxygen tubes in her shapely nose,
the one I wished I'd gotten,
she was still beautiful.
She had me write names
on things in the china closet.
I got a hand-painted plate from Bavaria,
long-haired cows on it.

The day she died I couldn't go into her room;
none of us could.
My father called an ambulance.
They took her to Mercy Hospital.
My youngest sister flew from Denver
with her week-old daughter,
didn't make it on time.

My oldest sister and I talked to the priest,

picked a plot under a huge oak tree
where flowers would not thrive.
The mortician showed us a white casket
lined with bubblegum pink satin
that matched the cat eye glasses
of the real-live dead woman in it.
We chose a plain box.

I regret giving away her shoes,
Cinderella slippers with a kitten heel,
transparent lucite studded with rhinestones,
sequined bow over the open toe.
At 4 and 5, my sister and I
clomped and danced in them,
can-cans swirling to Ravel's Bolero.

Her hands were strong and square,
used to scrubbing potatoes, kneading bread,
and playing piano.
She tightened bolts on B-52's,
factory work during the war,
when she worked next to our grandfather.

I hadn't gotten to a point in my life
where I was easy with my mother,
where we were two adults.
Instead, I learned to empty bedpans
during my breaks from school.
My second sister, a nurse,
moved home and took a night job.
Together, we managed.
Grocery shopping was an adventure—
the meals were awful.
I drove her to chemo, but wouldn't go in,
sat in the waiting room reading
while she struggled with buttons.

I dream I am a blue convertible.
My mother is driving.
Patsy Cline is on the radio.
She closes her eyes to sing along
and the car sails off a cliff
over the tops of the pine trees.
I wake before we hit bottom.

Barbara **Dahlberg** spent her childhood in the woods of northern Minnesota, moving to Pittsburgh at age 11. Always a visual artist, she found her voice with the Western Pennsylvania Writing Project in 2001, and honed her skills as a Madwomen in the Attic since 2009. An art teacher with the Pittsburgh Public Schools for 20 years, she retired in 2009. Diagnosed with stage 4 cancer in 2009 and given months to live, she now lives in the Regent Square area of Pittsburgh where she writes and creates art.

Her work has been published in the *Lascaux Prize 2016, Pittsburgh City Paper, Pittsburgh Post Gazette, Pittsburgh Poetry Review, U.S.1 Worksheets,* and *Voices from the Attic.* She won first prize in the *Public Poetry: Work* contest, was a reader on the radio program *Prosody* and performed in *Being...She Said 2014.*

CPSIA information can be obtained
at www.ICGtesting.com
Printed in the USA
BVHW032308140819
555745BV00003B/24/P